Celebrate Winter

All About
Animals
in Winter

by Martha E. H. Rustad

raintree
a Capstone company — publishers for children

Raintree is an imprint of Capstone Global Library Limited, a company incorporated in England and Wales having its registered office at 7 Pilgrim Street, London, EC4V 6LB – Registered company number: 6695582

www.raintree.co.uk
myorders@raintree.co.uk

Text © Capstone Global Library Limited 2016
The moral rights of the proprietor have been asserted.

Edited by Erika L. Shores
Designed by Cynthia Della-Rovere
Picture research by Tracy Cummins
Production by Tori Abraham

Printed and bound in China.

ISBN 978 1 4747 0309 3
19 18 17 16 15
10 9 8 7 6 5 4 3 2 1

British Library Cataloguing in Publication Data
A full catalogue record for this book is available from the British Library.

Acknowledgements
FLPA: Robert Canis, 9; Getty Images: John Cancalosi, 19; Shutterstock: ANRi Photo, 21, Critterbiz, 7, Eric Isselee, 3, Erni, 11, Kellis, 13, Malivan_Iuliia, 5, nialat, Cover, sellingpix, Design Element, stativius, 1, Zolran, 15; SuperStock: NHPA, 17.

Every effort has been made to contact copyright holders of material reproduced in this book. Any omissions will be rectified in subsequent printings if notice is given to the publisher.

All the internet addresses (URLs) given in this book were valid at the time of going to press. However, due to the dynamic nature of the internet, some addresses may have changed, or sites may have changed or ceased to exist since publication. While the author and publisher regret any inconvenience this may cause readers, no responsibility for any such changes can be accepted by either the author or the publisher.

Contents

Finding food

What do animals do in winter?

Birds visit a bird table.

They eat seeds.

Feathers puff up to stay warm.

An owl hunts mice.

It swallows them whole.

A deer scrapes bark.

It eats at dusk and dawn.

A fluffy fox hunts rabbits.

A squirrel stays in its nest.
It eats food it has stored.

Winter rest

Bats sleep in caves.

They rest all winter.

A frog sleeps underground.
A frog wakes in spring.

Bears sleep in dens.

A bear's heart beats slowly.

A ladybird hides under bark.

It crawls out in spring.

What do you do in winter?

Glossary

bark outer layer of a tree trunk

bird table table or other structure that holds food for birds; people put bird seed onto bird tables to feed birds in winter

den animal home

seed tiny plant part from which new plants grow

spring one of the four seasons of the year; spring is after winter and before summer

winter one of the four seasons of the year; winter is after autumn and before spring

Read more

Life Story of a Frog (Animal Life Stories), Charlotte Guillain (Raintree, 2014)

What Can Live in the Snow? (What Can Live There?), John-Paul Wilkins (Raintree, 2014)

Websites

www.naturedetectives.org.uk/winter/
Download winter wildlife ID sheets, pick up some great snowy-weather-game ideas and discover all the fun you can have with winter sticks!

www.wildlifewatch.org.uk/
Explore the Wildlife Trust's wildlife watch website and get busy this winter spotting interesting winter plants and animals living near by! Follow badger's blog for great wildlife spotting tips and some fascinating photographs.

Index